BUILDINGS & BACKGROUNDS

by Vernon Gibberd

Illustrated by the author

Published for The National Trust
by Dinosaur Publications Ltd
Over, Cambridge, Great Britain

© Vernon Gibberd 1979
ISBN 0/85122/173/4
Second Edition

Over the past two thousand years or so we have completely changed the British landscape by our farming methods and by our buildings. Now what was once largely forest land has been transformed into a complicated pattern of fields, woods, villages and towns.

Nature has been tamed, and man is very clearly in charge, if not always in control, of his surroundings.

Early Britons lived mostly in small communities, in wood-framed huts with log or mud walls and thatched roofs. These were often clustered together in clearings in the woodland. Even the Romans built in wood, choosing brick or stone only for their most important buildings.

When the Romans went back to Italy their buildings were vandalised by the native Britons who used the materials again for their own buildings.

Saxon Hut

Bodiam Castle, East Sussex

Although most of the old wooden buildings have long since fallen down or have been altered, many of the better constructed ones in stone, such as castles, churches and manor houses, have survived because they were built to last. Often they served as places of refuge against the wandering bands of robbers who made the countryside unsafe for many centuries. It was not until the Middle Ages that manor houses stopped being built as strongly as castles and became the kind of country house we know today.

When we look at these surviving buildings today we recognise them at once because of the massive walls and small window openings. Another thing they all seem to have in common is that they fit so well into their backgrounds. They really do appear to have become a part of the landscape almost as if they were meant to be there.

Welsh Cottage

If we think this is a good thing, and something we would like to see in our new buildings, then it is worth trying to find out why this should be. It is not just a question of style, because fashion in architecture, like fashion in everything else, is changing all the time and a Victorian cottage can sit as comfortably in its setting as an ancient church.

Ashdown House, Oxfordshire

The simplest reason is that these old buildings are so often made out of the very ground they stand on, from the most commonly available materials of all – stone, mud, flint and chalk. Think of the wonderful Cotswold villages and farms which have been built in the beautiful warm coloured stone which lies underneath them.

The commonest building material of all, brick, is after all simply clay baked in ovens to make easily-handled blocks, which can be placed on top of one another and held together by a cement made of two other common materials, lime and sand.

Bricks began to be used in those places where the natural woodlands had been cut down or where there was no natural stone. In the last hundred years or so transport has improved so much that bricks are taken all over the place, but before that they were very much a local product. You could have told what part of the country you were in just by looking at the houses. Each district had its own colour bricks and local builders often designed their own decorative patterns. The London area produced yellow bricks, then there are the greys and silvers of East Anglia, the lovely plum coloured ones from Kent and Sussex and the hard reds of the Midlands and the North. There used to be thousands of small brickworks up and down the country. When a farmer or gentleman in the eighteenth century wanted a barn or country house it was common for the builder to dig out a brick-field and "fire" the bricks he needed on the actual site.

Building an eighteenth-century house

Brick patterns

Lake District Farm

In some cases the builder used earth itself. It was not baked in a kiln but dug out and mixed with water and straw to bind it together. This material was then piled up into the walls, which had to be very thick. They were usually whitewashed to stop the rain from washing away the surface. Many houses and farm buildings were put up in this way and quite a number survive, particularly in the West Country. The typical thatched Devonshire cottage which you often see on calendars and tea cosies was built like this.

Not only walls, but roofs, too, tell us about the local geology. The dark Welsh hills give us shining black slates, greenish ones come from the Lake District and where there is no stone we find clay tiles and thatch. Sometimes shingles are used. These are wooden tiles, usually made out of cedar. A house built of materials, to hand will obviously fit in better with the scenery than one built of factory-made bricks or blocks, however cheap and useful these may be.

West Country Cob

It is hard for us now to picture just how perfectly matched architecture used to be with its surroundings. Even a century or so ago every building was put up in the local style, or vernacular as it is called, and with local materials, but later, things started to get mixed up. So we find red brick houses in the middle of stone country or next to plastered houses in Suffolk. ·

These newcomers sometimes look out of place, but today we are beginning to try and see that our new buildings are designed to be good neighbours, not only with one another but also with the fields or streets in which they stand.

In earlier times only rich people could afford to bring building materials from other parts of the country, or even from abroad. They generally did this deliberately to make their buildings look different, and to show off to their poorer neighbours.

What else makes a building a part of its background?
Funnily enough old age is a quality we much admire in architecture.
Buildings, like human beings and plants, grow old but show it in
a rather different way. We do not say that old people are more
beautiful than young ones, it is usually the other way round, but we
do sometimes say that they have more character. We may admire
the way old people have come through difficulties and hardship
without giving up. In other words they have survived, and while it
shows in their faces or the way they stand and walk, it is
nevertheless an achievement. It is the same way with buildings: to
have survived for hundreds of years is an achievement, and we like
to think of all the people who have lived or worked or worshipped
in them. It is always interesting too to see how each owner through
history has altered a building to suit his or her own needs or fancies.

We also have to admit that buildings can improve with age. Years of rain and wind, sunshine and frost will change their colours, shapes and textures. Occasionally, as with the soft sandstones which wear away, this is wholly harmful, but often it can be beautiful, as with old timbers and brickwork. We call this slow process weathering. Also buildings move with age. Roof-lines sag, foundations settle, floors gradually start to slope. As long as this movement does not make the building unsafe it can give a softer more attractive shape. In recent years new buildings seem to be built in harsh, angular lines. We seem to be trying to prevent them from growing old, and now that we are using so many new materials which do not weather well, the surfaces simply become dirty, which is not at all the same thing as weathering. The result is shabby buildings which look in need of a good scrub.

Arlington Row, Gloucestershire

Another important part of architecture, and landscape too in its own way, is something we call scale. Scale simply means measure, but when we apply it to architecture we mean something more like proportion, how the separate parts of a building relate to its whole. These parts are governed by the scale of man himself, the basis of all our architecture. We put up buildings in the first place to protect ourselves, or our animals or machinery, from the weather.

When we have to house giraffes, as you will see at the zoo, we build to their scale, and we put mice into tiny cages and not into kennels.

Giraffe House

All this will seem very obvious, but we all too often forget this in our new towns and villages. We usually find out when something is out of scale in a street when it is too late – the building or structure has been put up. In the same way a small bush in a front garden can grow up into a huge tree to dwarf the house. Again we say it is out of scale.

London Terrace House

Most buildings start with a scale of their own. They may not be particularly good buildings, but the chances are you will be able to see what the builder or architect wanted.

But buildings, more than most other works of art, are subject to later changes by new owners. Good stories are not usually rewritten by later writers. No one would want to add bits to a Constable painting. But buildings do get messed about with at different times and can all too easily become spoiled. Of course, this is bound to happen. We find an old house has no bathroom perhaps, so we put one in, and then have to find room for another bedroom, so we add one on at the back. We find the windows are too small, so we put in bigger ones, and so on.

18

Now if we take out a window which was divided into smaller panes, and put in a large sheet of glass in its place we may also say that the scale has been destroyed.

In the same way if we add a tiny new window in the front of a large building the same thing can happen. The sense of unity, of *oneness*, has been broken, just as much as if we were to pencil a moustache on to somebody's portrait.

For some reason we like order and symmetry in things, perhaps because we are more or less symmetrical ourselves. Symmetry means we can be divided into two similar halves. Flowers, fishes, birds, all things that grow share this same quality, but things which don't grow, like lakes, mountains, and clouds, are irregular, though we still like it when chance assembles them into some sort of pattern like a range of hills or a mackerel sky.

We certainly like order and pattern in our buildings, as we do with wallpapers and dress materials. We like the patterns on Elizabethan houses, formed out of the areas of white plaster between the wood uprights and beams. Why the eye should like some surfaces broken up in this way, and find some shapes and proportions more pleasant to look at than others is something designers have puzzled about for centuries. The Ancient Greeks thought they had discovered the perfect rectangle and based a whole system of proportion on it, which some architects have continued to use ever since. Artists have connected this scale with the proportions of man and other living things as well, like plants and sea shells.

Lower Brockhampton, Herefordshire

But to return to buildings in landscape, where does scale come in here? In our older buildings scale tended to look after itself. Even in the larger buildings the over-all scale is often small because they were built in simple units or blocks which a man, or a small group of men, could handle comfortably with simple lifting tackle. When you look closely at a huge cathedral you can see it is made up of lots of small parts. Our landscape itself is small scale, our hills mostly low and rounded, our fields small and protected with low hedges and fences.

We should not forget that much of what we may see as the natural beauty of old buildings came about by chance. Builders in those days only had "natural materials" to use so they developed a local way of building which put these to use in the best way. No doubt medieval builders would have used corrugated iron for their barns if it had been available! Our problem today is how to put up buildings which will be cheap and at the same time improve with age and keep the scale of our towns and countryside.

York Minster

Rules and regulations do not always help either. Various Building and Health Acts have been passed in the past hundred years or so, to improve our health and sanitation. Most of us no longer have to live in dark, wet hovels as poor people did in both towns and villages until quite recently. Our new houses are taller, with bigger rooms and windows, but all too often they fail to fit in as snugly into their background as their older neighbours. We need more than simply warm, light rooms with good sanitation to make us happy.

Sadly, many of the towns, villages and cottages which we admire so much from the past could not be built again today because of the new regulations which have been brought in. In Elizabethan and Georgian times, if you wished to build yourself a house, you chose a plot of land and went ahead and put it up. There was no need to worry about mains water, or electricity, or drains, because there were none anyway, nor did you need permission from the Council to build in the first place, as you do today.

As our society grows more and more complicated we have to accept more restrictions, but perhaps we should stop and ask ourselves how many more regulations we can afford to bring in. We do not want to condemn people to live in slums again, but packaging them up in sanitary little boxes, like battery hens, is no good alternative either.

Before the motor car and bulldozer were invented roads usually followed natural routes and so grew up along streams and fences and around the contours of hills. It was not essential for them to be straight when the only vehicles were horse driven and slow. Naturally enough buildings grew up along these roads and in particular at cross roads, where they formed the heart of some future village or town. Most of the busy centres of our biggest cities probably started as a cross roads or market place hundreds of years ago.

We like these natural groupings, often brought about by chance but now that we have motor traffic to cope with it is going to be even more difficult to achieve the haphazard look of these places which we find so attractive. We like roads to bend, but it is easier and cheaper to make them straight. We will have to be prepared to spend more money if we are to keep our new towns pleasant as well as practical.

It is really rather ridiculous to think that many a village street, protected by the local Council from being changed or pulled down because of its special character would be turned down by the same Council if someone wanted to build the same thing again today.

We must somehow decide what kind of surroundings we want and make our regulations fit *them* and not the other way round. We will have to think hard about how far we can let the motor car invade the places we live and work, and to what extent we can go on putting people higher and higher into the sky in tall buildings in order to save land. People often make the best out of less than perfect conditions, providing they have some measure of freedom. Perhaps the time has now come when we should think more of freedom and less about making new laws.

Thaxted, Essex

So far in this book we have talked about well mannered buildings which fit in well with their surroundings. To finish with let us think about something very different – buildings designed for show and delight.

After all we need these buildings just as much as we need three-bedroomed houses, or factories or schools. We seem to be in danger of not building show places with the same wonderful enthusiasm of our ancestors. They were not shy of putting fantasy and splendour into their structures.

We need such follies, as they are sometimes called, scattered about the country. Of course if all buildings were follies it would become very boring, but the odd curious or spectacular building can be very enjoyable.

Albert Memorial, London

Fonthill Abbey, Wiltshire

One of the biggest follies ever built was Fonthill Abbey, put up by an eccentric man called William Beckford in 1796. Sadly, it was badly constructed, and fell down after a few years because of poor foundations.

With these kind of buildings materials and scale do not matter, in fact the rules are there to be broken. The richer the better. Think of the Albert Memorial in London for example, that vast and ornate umbrella put up to protect the statute of Prince Albert from the weather. What a splendid sight it makes as we see it across Hyde Park.

Our great cathedrals, too, rise high above their towns. They were built to the glory of God, but also to the glory of their townspeople who raised money to put them up, and who wanted them to be higher and better than the cathedral in the next town. All over the country follies and monuments have been raised in honour of long forgotten events. But they are still with us today to enjoy and our country would be poorer without them.

We sometimes say that the money they cost would be better spent on more ordinary buildings like schools and hospitals, but if our ancestors had thought like that we would live in very dreary surroundings today.

You can also find self expression in quite small buildings, and in details like church gargoyles or cottage porches.

People who took pride in their work showed it in a great variety of ways and trades. It does not matter to us why they did it, we should be grateful that they took the trouble and have given us so much enjoyment. Doubtless many of them were vain and pretentious, but they had the courage of their convictions.

Let us hope we can have the courage of ours too, and bring a little more delight into our own buildings.

Folly Gatehouse, East Horsley, Surrey

PLACES AND BUILDINGS TO VISIT

Towns and Villages

Aldeburgh (Suffolk)
Bath (Avon)
Blandford (Dorset)
Bradford on Avon (Wiltshire)
Brighton (East Sussex)
Burford (Oxfordshire)
Buxton (Derbyshire)
Chester (Cheshire)
Chichester (Sussex)
Cockermouth (Cumbria)
Durham (County Durham)
Edinburgh (Strathclyde)

Harrogate (Yorkshire)
Lavenham (Suffolk)
Lincoln (Lincolnshire)
Llanidloes (Powys)
Ludlow (Shropshire)
Milton Abbas (Dorset)
Portmeirion (Gwynedd)
Richmond (Yorkshire)
Stamford (Lincolnshire)
St. Ives (Cornwall)
Tenby (Dyfed)
Thaxted (Essex)

Buildings

Albert Memorial (London)
Arlington Row (Gloucestershire)
Ashdown House (Oxfordshire)
Blackpool Tower (Lancashire)
Blenheim Palace (Oxfordshire)
Brighton Pavilion (East Sussex)
Bodiam Castle (East Sussex)
Calton Hill (Edinburgh, Strathclyde)
Castle Howard (Yorkshire)
Claremont (Surrey)
Compton Wynyates (Warwickshire)
Dyrham Park (Avon)
Egyptian House (Penzance, Cornwall)

Folly Gatehouse (East Horsley, Surrey)
House in the Clouds (Thorpeness, Suffolk)
Layer Marney (Essex)
Lindisfarne Castle (Northumberland)
Longleat (Wiltshire)
Lower Brockhampton (Herefordshire)
The Pagoda (Kew Gardens, London)
Petworth House (West Sussex)
Powis Castle (Welshpool, Powys)
Seaton Delaval (Northumberland)
Stourhead (Wiltshire)
York Minster (Yorkshire)

65p net (UK only)

Made in Great Britain.
Printed by Tabro Litho, St. Ives, Cambs.
Reproduction by C. L. Enterprises, Fenstanton, Cambs.
Bound by Suffolk Print Finishers, Bury St. Edmunds.